Introductio

The Yoga Sutras of Patanjali is the most influential and authoritative text ever written in the history of the yoga tradition. It is the foundation for all of the various schools, branches, and sects of yoga that appeared after its writing sometime around 200 BC. In my tradition of Kriya Yoga, it is considered the most important philosophical discourse regarding yoga, samkhya, meditation, and enlightenment. The text is divided into four parts or chapters called Padas. The first chapter, Samadhi Pada, is the most definitive and essential, and it is the subject of this book.

I have done my utmost to adhere to the original Sanskrit in my translation of Samadhi Pada. I painstakingly read and studied several different translations by famous Sanskrit scholars and used my own discernment to arrive at the most logical and precise English version of Patajali's original teachings. However, no two scholars can agree on the exact translation of many important Sanskrit terms used by Patanjali and I am sure there will be areas of disagreement regarding my own translation and interpretation. This is unavoidable. However, the reader can rest assured that I have spent countless hours contemplating each sutra (verse) in excruciating detail in our ashram here in the powerful and majestic southern Andes Mountains of Chile.

The Yoga Sutras is not meant to be read quickly or in one sitting. The reader is invited to read this translation and commentary slowly and methodically. In fact, I highly recommend reading only one or two verses a day. After reading each verse, the reader should sit in the silence and contemplate the deep and profound meaning of each verse until an insight or revelation occurs. This is the proper way to study the sacred scriptures of all spiritual traditions. In this way, the study of sacred scripture becomes a meditative and contemplative practice, rather than a mere intellectual exercise.

Samadhi Pada

1.1 Now, the teachings of Yoga begin.

There exists a subtle implication in the first verse of the Yoga Sutras of Patanjali. The word "now" is auspicious and profound in this context. The intuited implication is that one was not ready for the teachings of Yoga prior to picking up this text. However, "now," one *is* ready. The reader has reached a state of preparedness to embark on a spiritual journey of learning and comprehension that they were not ready for previously. This is the beginning of the path to awakening, oneness consciousness, and final liberation. The inner pilgrimage to soul-freedom, which every sentient being in the universe ultimately craves, is about to be explained.

1.2 Yoga is the cessation of the vrittis in our being.

This is the most important verse in the history and philosophy of Yoga because it provides us with the most authoritative definition of the word yoga given in any ancient yoga text. The verse in Sanskrit is, "yoga-chitta-vritti-nirodha." It is useful to know the specific meaning of each word in this verse in order to fully comprehend its profound meaning.

Yoga is commonly defined as the union of atman (soul) with Brahman (God). In the Yoga Sutras, yoga also means samadhi; they are synonyms according to Patanjali. In samadhi there is no distinction between subject and object. Subject and object cease to exist in the experience of samadhi. There is only a oneness beyond description.

It is an ineffable mystical experience that cannot be explained via verbiage. The yogi must experience samadhi (yoga) in order to understand and know it. It is beyond all intellectual knowledge. Any attempt to understand samadhi with the intellect is futile. The intellect operates within a dualistic framework, which is completely transcended in samadhi. Many sincere yogis practice yoga and meditation for decades without a single experience of samadhi. Likewise, many well intentioned yogis believe that they have experienced samadhi when, in all actuality, they have not. Many sincere, albeit misguided, spiritual teachers believe that samadhi is merely a peaceful, objective, thought-free state of superconsciousness. However, this is simply not the case.

Chitta is typically translated as mind or consciousness. However, this common mistranslation falls short. The chitta should be understood as comprising our entire being with all its layers. In the cosmology of yoga, there exist five dimensions or layers of our being known as pancha kosha (the five koshas). The koshas, or sheaths, are said to "cover up" our atman, or soul. This is, of course, impossible, as the soul has no vibratory reality and it therefore cannot be covered. The soul is omnipresent and exists everywhere, or nowhere, depending upon one's point of view. It is possible to experience distracting vibrations or fluctuations (vrittis) in every layer of our being. Therefore, we should not limit our definition of chitta to merely include the mind. For example, when one is attempting to meditate and there is physical discomfort or pain in the annamaya kosha (the physical body), they are experiencing vrittis at the level of the physical body. When one experiences energetic or emotional distractions, these are occuring in the pranamaya kosha (the astral body). When one experiences distracting thoughts and memories, these vibratory phenomena are occurring in the manomaya kosha (the mind). When one experiences their ego-self or false identity, these vrittis occur on the level of the vijnanamaya kosha (the ego). Finally, when one experiences the vibratory phenomena of spiritual ecstasy, these vrittis or distractions occur within the anandamaya kosha (the bliss sheath). If the mind were the only obstacle to overcome, Patanjali would not have included techniques (the eight limbs/steps of yoga) for overcoming obstacles (vrittis) in every kosha.

Vrittis, as I have just explained, are vibratory phenomena that distract us from experiencing our true Self as pure, unbounded, infinite, loving consciousness. They occur in every layer of our being. Through the various techniques of yoga, we can learn to calm and pacify vrittis so that we can experience our true nature that has no vrittis or vibrational reality. Patanjali explains each technique, or step, in the yoga process in the second section of the Sutras.

Nirodha is simply the cessation or pacification of the fluctuations that distract the yogi during meditation. There are eight steps or techniques given by Patanjali later in the text that assist in the cessation of vrittis. These eight steps are a logical scientific process that, when practiced correctly, can result in superconscious states and ultimately, samadhi.

1.3 Then, the observer abides in its own nature.

When the observer exists without distracting observations, it can simply be as it is without modification. Our true nature as pure existence-being exists outside the bounds of space and time and all vibratory, manifest phenomena. The Self is a oneness that exists beyond subject-object duality. There are no words that can aptly describe it. The great mystical poets of every age have tried through their lofty and esoteric descriptions to depict the Self, and all have failed. We must experience our true nature directly to fully understand it. There is no other way. Therefore, the idea that there are many paths to God is erroneous. There is truly only one path; we must abide as the Self. There is nothing else.

1.4 Otherwise, there is identification with vrittis.

When one is not in samadhi, they identify with the false self, which is composed of vrittis. Typically we tend to identify with the body-mind-personality composite, or false self. This error in identification is the source of all our problems, ignorance, and suffering. Yoga is the process by which we can reverse this error and experience enlightenment. We believe that we are that which suffers; therefore, we suffer. We are, instead, the observer of that which suffers. The observer is incapable of suffering. It is pure, unbounded consciousness that observes all vibratory phenomena from a "place" of complete, placid, tranquil peace and stillness. It does not vibrate, move, change, suffer, or die. It is forever peaceful, still, content, and whole. It requires nothing and desires nothing. Therefore, we never actually suffer. Suffering is an illusion caused by an error in identification and nothing more. Once we sever our identification with the body-mind-personality composite, we experience what we actually are, and we end our suffering for a time until we become identified again with the false, limited, separate self.

In the philosophy of yoga the manifest universe of form is known to be a grand illusion called maya. All vibratory phenomena are constantly changing and impermanent. Therefore, the vibratory realm is not real in the truest sense of the word. The only "thing" that is real is the Self, which does not change and is eternal. The Self does not vibrate and is incapable of change. For something to change, it must vibrate. Every waveform has a beginning and an end. The Self had no beginning and will have no end. It is what it is and will always be what it is. We are that.

1.5 There are five kinds of mental vrittis, which are either painful or painless.

There are several types of vrittis that occur in the mental field. Some of them cause pain, while others do not.

1.6 They are accurate knowledge, misperception, conceptualization, sleep and memory.

Mental vrittis modify the mind leading to experiences of pleasure and/or pain. When we begin to experience dispassionate objectivity during refined superconscious states, we realize that pleasure and pain are two sides of the same coin and there is really no difference between them. When we stop chasing after pleasure and avoiding pain, we experience a deep and lasting peace. Pleasure creates attachments and pain creates aversions. Neither attachments nor aversions are useful on the spiritual path. Both result in restlessness, suffering, further identification with the false self, and reincarnation into form.

1.7 The means of acquiring accurate knowledge are direct perception, inference, and testimony.

A spiritual seeker can gain knowledge on their quest by means of direct experience, inference and intuition, and the testimony and teachings of enlightened or semi-enlightened teachers. The most accurate knowledge comes about by direct experience. However, in the beginning of our path, direct experience is usually lacking. Likewise, in the beginning, due to a lack of discernment (viveka), we also struggle to gain knowledge via our intuition. It typically requires years of disciplined practice to sharpen the mind in order to gain accurate knowledge via inference and/or intuition. Therefore, we generally require information and knowledge gained via the teachings of a wise and experienced Guru, especially in the beginning.

All of the classical yoga texts authenticate the vital role of the Guru on the spiritual journey. Learning from a wise teacher who is at the very least semi-enlightened is an essential part of the awakening path. The Guru provides us with a map that can guide us to our ultimate destination. Otherwise, we are likely to wander around aimlessly and end up lost in the woods of spiritual confusion. This is the fate of the vast majority of seekers, especially in the egoic-minded West, who have decided that the Guru is an antiquated phenomenon. The Guru-disciple relationship has worked for thousands of years and will continue to work well into the future. Spiritual laws do not change just because societies and cultures change. Spiritual laws come from a higher, elevated order and have nothing whatsoever to do with ever-changing human societies and cultures on this particular planet at this particular time. Universal spiritual laws are not governed by space and time, as many superficial, misguided seekers would have us believe. Until we begin to have our own direct experiences of the Divine, the accurate knowledge gained via the testimony of the Guru is necessary and invaluable. It cannot and should not be underestimated by those willful seekers looking to go it alone in their current incarnation.

1.8 Misperception is false knowledge based upon illusions.

Misperception of what is observed results in illusions that cause irrational thinking. Illusions lead to confusion on behalf of the truth seeker. The primary illusion impeding our enlightenment is a flawed sense of self-identity. When this error is corrected, our awareness is restored to its natural state. The highest objective of spiritual practice is to transcend the illusional sense of self in order to experience our true Self as pure, loving, non-dual existence-being in samadhi.

1.9 Conceptualization relies on words, which are not the objects themselves.

Words are mental constructs and labels that attempt to describe objects. However, they are not the objects themselves. I can describe a beautiful beach in Florida in great detail, and one can form a mental concept of the beach, but this concept can never replicate the experience of being on the beach and directly experiencing the sights, smells, sensations, sounds, etc. Likewise, the great sages can describe their mystical experiences, but we must have our own experiences to have real knowledge of the Divine. Words simply do not do justice in describing mystical experiences and they never prove satisfactory for one wishing to know the Divine oneself.

Yoga is a mystical tradition and not a religion. Mystical traditions differ from religious traditions in important ways. For example, in mystical traditions we wish to have direct experience of the Divine rather than having religious beliefs about the Divine. Religions have their basis in beliefs about the Divine, whereas mystical traditions have their basis in direct experience of the Divine. My Guru, Roy Eugene Davis, often said, "Don't be a believer. Be a knower!" Beliefs do not satisfy us at our spiritual core. They leave an epistemological void that can only be filled by direct, mystical experience.

1.10 Sleep is a mental vritti that produces an unconscious state.

Until we have learned how to sleep superconsciously, sleep is largely an unconscious experience. Sometimes, during periods of deep, dreamless sleep, vrittis cease. However, because we are unconscious, we are not aware of the experience. Meditation provides us with an opportunity to be fully aware of the nirodha state of the vrittis. This superconscious state differs greatly from the unconscious state of sleep.

It is also possible to experience a trance state while we are awake that is somewhat similar to the deep, dreamless sleep state. However, in a trance state we are likewise largely unconscious. In fact, when people go into a trance state they tend to forget what happened while they were in that state. While in trance, it is possible to experience a temporary cessation of thoughts, but this is because one has ventured "below" the mind. In a superconscious state, we experience ourselves as superior to the mind or "above" the mind. This difference has been erroneously described by some spiritual teachers as a "subtle difference." The difference between trance and superconsciousness is not subtle at all; it is like night and day. The confusion of inexperienced spiritual teachers only creates more confusion in their students and followers. As Jesus said, "It is the blind leading the blind."

1.11 Memory is the inability of the objects of experience to escape.

Memories are vrittis that modify the mind and cause identification with previous experiences. They have the ability to cause pleasure or pain depending upon our attachments and/or aversions to them. Like all vrittis, memories should be observed objectively without reaction, judgment, participation, or identification. We are not our memories, or any other vritti for that matter. Memories should be treated as files that can be accessed when necessary and nothing more. Memories are important in that they orient us in time. Without them, we would have no sense of time and it would be impossible to function normally as a body/mind/personality composite.

1.12 The cessation of vrittis occurs by practice and non-attachment.

For one to become proficient in anything in life, they must be willing to practice diligently; yoga is no different. The difference in meditative proficiency between someone who has meditated daily for fifty years and someone who is just beginning on the path is like the difference between a highly skilled professional athlete in their prime and a child who has just picked up a ball for the first time. In our modern technological society, instant gratification has become more insidious than at any other time in human history. This trend does not bode well for those of us who teach meditation. As attention spans grow ever shorter, it is becoming increasingly difficult to convince people to sit still and concentrate for five minutes, let alone an hour (which is the minimum time recommended for deep, profound meditative experiences). There is no substitute for disciplined daily practice and there are no shortcuts. Seekers must be willing to practice; there is no alternative.

Non-attachment is an essential part of the yoga path. However, it is often misunderstood by many seekers to mean renunciation or monkhood. One need not give away all their belongings and move alone to the forest, forgoing family, career, and a normal worldly life. This is a superficial comprehension of non-attachment. What *is* necessary is the renunciation of our attachments and aversions. This does not require that we live in a cave, ashram, or monastery. However, it is recommended for a yogi to live a simple lifestyle with few possessions, but a simple lifestyle is not necessarily a prerequisite for a yogi. There are a few examples of wealthy individuals who have become advanced yogis. Non-attachment is an internal process, and has little to do with anything external. A simple lifestyle is recommended because it provides fewer opportunities for financial stress, possessiveness, materialism, over-consumption, and greed. As of the writing of this book in 2021, the planet is dangerously polluted and many species are quickly becoming extinct. It is the responsibility of every seeker to leave as small a footprint on the planet as possible to preserve this planet/university for future generations of souls that will incarnate here to learn, grow, and evolve towards Self-realization.

1.13 Meditation practice is the maintenance of being there.

What does it mean to "be there?" For anyone who has ever "been there," no further explanation of this simple verse is required. However, for one who has not experienced it, "being there" is the experience of abiding as the Self in perfect unity, peace, stillness, and tranquility. Meditation is the core practice of yoga. Without it, one cannot be said to be practicing yoga. In the Western world, yoga has become associated primarily with physical postures and stretching exercises. While these physical practices are highly beneficial and health-promoting, they do not represent the full practice of yoga. The ancient yogis gave very little importance to asanas, or physical postures. Of primary importance for the original rishis and yogis was meditation practice. As we can clearly see in the first chapter of the most important yogic text ever written, there is no mention of asana, but there *is* mention of meditation and samadhi.

1.14 Meditation becomes firmly grounded by devoted, uninterrupted practice.

According to my Guru, who had approximately sixty years of experience teaching meditation and who initiated more than fifteen thousand devotees in Kriya Yoga, only approximately ten percent of his students and initiates continued to meditate after they learned how. Of this ten percent, he told me that only a few hundred truly benefited from the meditation methods that he taught. There are verses in other ancient yoga texts such as the Bhagavad Gita, which state that only a tiny percentage of people truly seek the Divine, and of this tiny percentage only an even tinier percentage possess the discipline and devotion necessary to experience samadhi, enlightenment, and moksha (liberation). Having taught for a decade myself, I can attest to this from my own personal experience as a spiritual teacher. Many seekers mistakenly assume that they can meditate occasionally or when they feel like it and derive benefit from their sadhana (spiritual practices).

Neuroplasticity is the process by which our brain reroutes neural connections and reshapes itself. This process is always occuring, even into old age. Daily, disciplined meditation practice is the process of rewiring the brain in order to facilitate elevated and enlightened states of consciousness. Enlightenment, in no small part, is a physiological process. This process of enlightened neuroplasticity requires years of uninterrupted practice and diligence. Reading books and/or watching videos about enlightenment will not rewire and prepare the brain for enlightenment; only meditation has this capacity. It is useful to educate oneself intellectually, but there is no substitute for superconscious meditation in the enlightenment process. Tapas, or discipline, is the key to unlocking one's hidden and dormant spiritual potential. Without it, seekers generally struggle for decades floating from one spiritual tradition to the next without any noticeable spiritual progress. These seekers could have saved decades of wasted time, energy, and resources by simply learning to sit still and quiet the mind.

1.15 Non-attachment is the mastery of not clinging to the objects of desires, both seen and heard.

Objects themselves do not cause desires. Clinging to objects causes desires. The relationships that we have with objects are the cause of all our attachments and aversions (karma). When we are attached to something and we cannot have it, we suffer. When we are averse to something, and it is in our presence, we suffer. Therefore, attachments and aversions only lead to suffering. This is a universal truth widely accepted in many religious and spiritual traditions. We must cultivate neutrality and objectivity as it concerns the relationships we have with objects to avoid creating attachments and aversions.

When we react to something positively, we create attachments. Likewise, when we react to something in a negative manner, we create aversions. Therefore, reactions are the root of all suffering and karma. Dispassionate objectivity is necessary to avoid reactivity. When objects are viewed neutrally and objectively without reaction, we do not create any new karma via our attachments and aversions. We learn how to cultivate dispassionate objectivity with a daily superconscious meditation practice. However, we must also learn to practice non-attachment at all times; not only while we are meditating. This requires constant vigilance and persistence. In the Buddhist tradition, this practice is erroneously called "mindfulness." A more precise and appropriate name for this practice is "objective observation." A serious seeker on the path must learn how to observe all changing and impermanent phenomena objectively without judgment, reaction, participation, or identification. We are not that which is observed or observable; we are, instead, the observer.

1.16 A higher form of non-attachment is not clinging to the gunas due to the knowledge of purusha.

The cosmology of triguna (the three gunas) derives from the Samkhya philosophy of ancient India. The gunas are vibratory forces in the manifest realm that are responsible for all of creation. From the Om vibration, which is considered the primordial vibration emanating from the unmanifest, come the three gunas of sattva, rajas, and tamas. Every waveform/vibration possesses three constituent parts: a trough, a rising/descending action, and a peak. The trough of the primordial om vibration creates a vibratory force known as tamas guna that is associated with density, heaviness, dullness, and low states of consciousness. The rising and descending actions of the om vibration create a vibratory force known as rajas guna, which is associated with activity, action, stimulation, and restless states of consciousness. The peak of the om vibration creates a vibratory force known as sattva guna, which is associated with elevation, lightness, and enlightened states of consciousness.

God is one thing. However, it has two facets; one manifest and one unmanifest. We can think of the two facets of God as two sides of the same coin. The manifest realm of vibratory form is known as prakriti, which is created via the interactions of om and the three gunas. The unmanifest is known as purusha. It is formless, omnipotent, omnipresent, and omniscient. When one has gained knowledge of purusha via direct experience, one can use their powers of viveka (discernment) to differentiate between the manifest and unmanifest easily. Prior to direct experience of purusha, discernment is merely an intellectual exercise, albeit a very useful one. However, once one has experienced purusha directly, viveka becomes automatic and effortless.

1.17   Lesser superconscious states are mixed with reasoning, contemplation, bliss, and ego identification.

It is possible to experience inferior superconscious states that are mixed with subtle thoughts, sensations of bliss, and a lingering sense of separateness and individuality.   This is what most meditators experience during the "peak experience" of their meditations for the first year or so of practice (many meditators never go beyond this stage).   It is a useful superconscious stage, as one begins to experience a sense of being superior to the body, mind, personality, and ego. However, vrittis remain and must ultimately be transcended in order to reach the next stage of superconscious awareness, which is a superconsciousness free of distracting vrittis described in the following verse.   However, neither of these stages of superconsciousness is samadhi. Many misinterpretations of the Yoga Sutras have created untold amounts of confusion regarding these two verses. What is described by Patanjali in these two verses are two preliminary stages of superconsciousness, but not samadhi.

1.18   True superconsciousness is thought-free, leaving behind residual samskaras.

I have heard many modern meditation teachers proclaim that meditation is not a thought-free state, and that it is impossible to stop the steady stream of thoughts in the mind. They tell us that we are to merely observe our thoughts, rather than try to stop them entirely. The objective observation of our thoughts is useful and should be practiced all day every day.   However, mindfulness (objective observation) is not meditation.   Prolonged thought-free meditative states are, in fact, possible to experience, usually after years of ardent practice.   Thought-free superconsciousness is dhyana, or authentic meditation.

When we experience the stillness of thought-free superconsciousness, we are given our first glimpse of our true nature as pure, infinite, loving consciousness.   In the stillness, many beneficial things start to occur in the various layers of our being. For example, we start to hear/feel the subtle om vibration, we start to see an inner light (jyoti) in the ajna chakra, and we start to produce soma (divine nectar) in the brain. All of these inner changes are important steps on our way to enlightenment, and they all begin to occur in thought-free states of superconscious stillness. These inner changes leave behind mental and/or energetic impressions known as samskaras.

Samskaras are of two basic types; useful and non-useful. They are similar to memories, but memories are but one example of samskaras. When we have an experience, there is a residual impression left behind in our being that creates a vibratory imprint following the experience. These imprints (samskaras) stay with us and affect our future experiences. A samskara is useful if it assists us on our spiritual path towards awakening. A samskara is non-useful if it impedes or retards our progress. Hearing the om vibration, seeing the inner light, producing soma nectar, resting in the profound stillness...all of these superconscious experiences leave behind useful samskaras that prepare us for the various stages of samadhi and assist us in our spiritual evolution.

As yogis, we ought to make a conscious effort to cultivate useful samskaras and cease participating in those activities and experiences that produce non-useful samskaras. This does not necessarily mean that one must live alone in a cave eschewing all social contact in an attempt to avoid all non-useful samskaras (although, there is certainly nothing wrong with that). However, one is advised to live as simple a life as possible with minimal social interactions even if one is a householder yogi living in the world. My Guru, for example, had what he referred to as a "semi-monastic" lifestyle. I have followed his lead in my own life, and it has proven highly beneficial.

1.19 There is a tendency to return to body-consciousness following a period of profound superconsciousness.

Superconscious states do not last. They are not permanent. One must consistently cultivate superconsciousness on a daily basis in order to sustain it. There are a few rare Masters who have attained a sort of permanent superconsciousness, but they are few and far between. They serve as pole stars for the rest of us to follow on our journey to self-mastery. Most of us must do the daily work of sadhana, tending to the garden of our being. Each and every day, we must pull the weeds of unwholesome thoughts and desires, add the fertilizer of superconscious and sattvic influences, water the blossoming flowers with the purity of our essence, and expose our entire garden to the sunlight of God's amazing grace. In doing so, we prepare the soil and cultivate our garden-being so that superconsciousness becomes more and more influential in our day to day lives.

1.20 Through faith, strength, contemplation, and wisdom, others experience samadhi.

The overwhelming majority of seekers never experience samadhi. In fact, most seekers are lucky if they ever experience a prolonged state of thought-free superconsciousness. I have friends who have reported to me that they have been meditating in a disciplined way for more than forty years and have never had a single experience of samadhi. I have a deep respect for these friends because they are persistent and unrelenting in their pursuit of oneness consciousness, and they continue to benefit greatly from their daily meditation practice. In this verse, Patanjali is letting us know that if we wish to go beyond preliminary superconscious states to the various stages of samadhi, we must practice with faith, strength, contemplation, and wisdom. If we are not born with these distinguished traits, they may be cultivated via self-control, will power, and the guidance of a wise Guru.

1.21 For intense practitioners, it is near.

Samadhi is our natural state. Therefore, it is a paradox that one must practice intensively to experience it. If we already are that, then why is practice of any kind necessary to experience that which we already are?   There are so many movements, changes, fluctuations, modifications, and vibrations occurring in our being that we become identified with all of these vrittis. When the vrittis are pacified, we have an opportunity to experience our true nature in the tranquil stillness. Yoga is the process by which we pacify vrittis so that our true nature is uncovered. Enlightenment is an uncovering, not an attainment. However, in order to uncover our eternal core, we must engage in practices and techniques that neutralize and pacify the vrittis occuring in the coverings (koshas) that distract us from simply abiding as the Self.

There are popular teachers within the Advaita Vedanta tradition that do not recommend any meditation practices. They encourage their students to simply "be present" and abide as the Self. We should not be surprised to see the current mass exodus of their students to systems that provide *useful* and practical meditation techniques, rather than *useless* pronouncements and pontifications.

There are many reincarnated yogis who have already been meditating for many lifetimes who do not require as intense a practice as novices.   Therefore, an "intense practice" will look different for different people.   There is no one-size-fits-all sadhana.   In the following verse, three levels of intensity are listed.

1.22 Progress depends on the level of intensity, which is either mild, moderate, or extreme.

Generally, the more one meditates, the more quickly they awaken spiritually. I have seen this with my own students. Those whose commitment is firm and steady tend to experience rapid progress on the path. Likewise, those whose practice is inconsistent and lackadaisical tend to progress very slowly. The same can be said for learning how to play a musical instrument or learning a new language. These things require commitment, discipline, devotion, and maturity. What half-hearted seekers fail to comprehend is the brevity of life. We are only given a certain number of days on this planet in this current form. We must make the most of every precious moment we are given without exception. If spiritual evolution is not one's top priority, then they are wasting their life performing largely frivolous and meaningless activities.

1.23 Or by surrender to Ishvara.

The phrase used by Patanjali in this verse is "Ishvara-pranidhana." Pranidhana is typically translated as surrender or devotion. Ishvara is far more complicated to translate. It has a wide array of meanings and interpretations. However, as it is used by Patanjali, I have come to understand it as that aspect of the supreme consciousness that guides our spiritual evolution. Meister Eckhart, a medieval Christian mystic, spoke in his famous sermons about the importance of emptying our own will and replacing it with the will of God. I believe this is what Patanjali is referring to here. We must, in essence, empty ourselves of ourselves and open our being to the inflowing grace of Divine guidance and transformation.

Many have mistakenly interpreted this verse to mean something akin to Bhakti Yoga (the yoga of devotion). However, the yoga described in the Yoga Sutras of Patanjali is Raja Yoga (the path of sadhana and meditation). Therefore, I do not believe that Patanjali was referring to Bhakti Yoga. I believe he was describing the hollowing out of our ego to make way for the flow of Divine grace. By removing the primary obstacle to the flow (ego), we open the gates of our being to receive the enlightening transmissions of guidance, direction, catalyzation, and blessings from the Divine intelligence. Pranidhana is better translated as "surrendering to the will/flow of...," rather than simply surrender or devotion. Therefore, Ishvara pranidhana truly means surrendering ourselves to the will/flow of that aspect of the supreme consciousness that guides our spiritual evolution.

1.24 Ishvara is the supreme purusha, unaffected by the kleshas or karma.

While Ishvara is the root cause of manifestation, it is unaffected by the happenings within manifestation. What is true of the macrocosm is also true of the microcosm; as above, so below. Therefore, as individualized units of the supreme consciousness, we are likewise unaffected by the happenings within manifestation. Nothing ever happens to us. Any suffering we experience occurs within the koshas and never occurs at the level of pure consciousness. Therefore, in reality, we never suffer. The soul has no karma. It is always and forever pure. This is where the philosophy of yoga truly differs from that of the Judeo-Christian tradition. In the Western religions, we are taught that we are inherently sinful and debased due to the original sin of Eve in the Garden of Eden. In the yoga tradition, we discover that we are inherently Divine. There is no more vitally important distinction to be drawn between the two systems. One is life-negating and self-defeating, while the other one is true.

Kleshas are afflictions, or the causes of suffering in the philosophy of yoga. Karma is our accumulated attachments and aversions that are responsible for our habits, patterns, tendencies, etc. The soul is free from the effects of the kleshas and karma. The observer remains unaffected by its observations. Only when the mind intervenes does one react, identify, judge, and participate. When the mind is still, the observer observes without the interference of vrittis. This is our natural state.

1.25 There, the seed of omniscience is unsurpassed.

Enlightened beings are omniscient. In the stillness of our pure essence, all is known. This does not mean that an enlightened person necessarily possesses a lot of worldly knowledge. Enlightenment has little to do with the memorization of facts pertaining to this particular planet and its human inhabitants. The knowledge gained via enlightenment experiences is of a much higher order and magnitude. The promise of meditation practice is the acquisition of knowledge regarding our true, eternal nature. This knowledge can only be gained via direct experience in deep meditation; there is no other way.

1.26 That, being unlimited by time, is also the Guru of the ancients.

Paramahansa Yogananda, my Guru's Guru, frequently said, "God is the real Guru. I am just his representative." That aspect of the supreme consciousness that subtly guides our spiritual evolution and unfoldment is the true Guru. It is the Guru of all the Gurus. There is no higher teacher. If one has not yet reached the requisite level of spiritual maturity necessary for working with an embodied Guru in their current incarnation, they can rest assured that they will receive inner guidance from the primordial Guru, Ishvara.

1.27 The expression of that is pranava.

Pranava, or om, is the primordial vibration. It is the substratum out of which all of manifestation unfolds. In the Bible, it is referred to as the logos or the word. In the yoga tradition, om is thought to be evidence of the Divine as its first expression. There is no more subtle vibratory frequency in the universe. All other vibratory frequencies ultimately emanate from om. It is the closest that we can get to the formless within the world of form.

1.28 The repetition of it unveils its meaning.

The repetition of om is an example of mantra practice. However, this is not what Patanjali is referring to in this verse. What he is actually describing is the contemplation of the primordial vibration itself, and not the mental repetition of the word "om" used as a mantra. Mantra has its place and is an effective form of concentration (dharana). Notwithstanding, the contemplation of om, also referred to as Nada Yoga or Shabda Yoga, is considered the highest practice of dharana, and is superior to ordinary mantra practice.

One should begin their practice by focusing their attention on the subtle sounds occurring in the head, such as the sound of blood flow and/or the electrical signals produced in the brain. Once one's concentration and attention are fully focused on this physical sound, they should search with minimal effort for a more subtle sound frequency, and so on and so forth until they experience the om vibration. Once one is experiencing the om vibration, they should unite their attention so completely with om that they experience themselves as om. This is an example of savikalpa samadhi, or union with support. This is a very advanced technique and usually requires many years of disciplined practice to master.

1.29 Through this practice, the immutable Self is revealed and obstacles are removed.

Listening for om is known as omkar kriya in my tradition of Kriya Yoga. When we practice omkar, which is the same as shabda or nada, we attempt to align our attention and awareness entirely with the primordial vibration. If we succeed in doing so, our false identification is removed from our body/mind/personality composite and we instead identify ourselves with the om vibration for a time. While this experience of savitarka samadhi (samadhi with the support of an object of contemplation) is important and useful, it is not entirely transformative. Experiencing ourselves as the om vibration is interesting and it allows us a glimpse of ego-loss, but it is not union with the Self. In order to experience nirvitarka samadhi (unsupported samadhi), we must go beyond the stage of union with om to "reveal the immutable Self." This experience of true samadhi is possible via the use of omkar kriya, but it is incredibly rare and requires years of diligent, unceasing practice. Therefore, when Patanjali states, "Through this practice, the immutable Self is revealed and obstacles are removed," he is implying that it must be practiced for many years with discipline.

The enlightenment process is an extremely long journey that most likely never ends. There are a few rare exceptions of people who have awakened fully via a powerful instantaneous enlightenment experience. We can probably count them all on both hands in the entire history of the world. Most of us experience a long, slow, gradual, evolutionary process as we grow towards enlightenment. The yoga path is not for the half-hearted or feeble. It requires great commitment, devotion, surrender, and self-control.

1.30 Distractions that occur in our being are disease, apathy, doubt, carelessness, laziness, sense pleasure cravings, false perception, failure to attain a firm basis in yoga, and restlessness.

These distractions become obstacles for one whose goal is samadhi and spiritual illumination. For one who is not intent on awakening, these distractions are simply a part of daily life. Very little thought is given to overcoming or transcending these impediments for ordinary people stuck in auto-pilot. However, for a yogi, these distractions/obstacles must be dealt with if they wish to experience elevated and enlightened states of consciousness and being.

Disease may be prevented by adhering to a healthy Ayurvedic lifestyle routine. Apathy should be replaced with enthusiasm for the spiritual awakening path. Doubt should be replaced with faith in the Divine. Carelessness should be replaced with constant vigilance and alertness. Laziness should be replaced by a commitment to hard work based upon the inspiration of the wise Masters and Gurus who have experienced what we wish to experience. Sense pleasure cravings must be replaced by contentment and peace via a dedicated superconscious meditation practice and dispassionate non-attachment. False perceptions must be replaced by accurate perceptions using our powers of discernment. Failure to attain a firm basis in yoga must be replaced by a daily yoga and meditation practice. Restlessness should be replaced by stillness, which only comes about as a result of a regular superconscious meditation practice. In short, meditation is the solution for overcoming all of the distractions/obstacles listed in this verse.

1.31 The distractions are accompanied by suffering, depression, restlessness of the body, and irregular breathing.

Until we have accomplished total self-mastery, we suffer the effects of identifying with a body, mind, and personality. This is the ordinary human condition; a life of suffering and ignorance. On the other hand, the promise of the spiritual path is a life of peace, knowledge/experience of the Divine, and bliss. Intense suffering is not a prerequisite for embarking on the spiritual path, but it very often precedes it. Many seekers begin practicing yoga and meditation as a way to escape pain. While this is a tamasic motivation for starting on the spiritual path, it ultimately has a sattvic result. However, a better approach is to seek the Divine with a completely selfless attitude. In this way, we do not enter onto the path with selfish motivations from the beginning. We should always try and practice in a selfless manner for the benefit of all beings everywhere. We must realize that if we practice in a selfish manner, the self that we are practicing for is constantly changing, fleeting, and impermanent. This self that we think we are eventually dies. However, by practicing in a selfless manner, we realize that it is far better to focus on the healing, peace, and enlightenment of all beings in every dimension of the vibratory multiverse to ensure the elevation and purification of the non-local collective consciousness that we share with everyone everywhere. In doing so, we play our role in the evolutionary impulses of the Divine, leading to the quickening of global enlightenment and planetary peace.

1.32   Single-pointed concentration upon an object is the means for preventing these distractions.

Superconscious states are commonly experienced following the concentration of our attention and awareness upon a single object, such as the om vibration, an internal light in the third eye, a visualized yantra (sacred geometrical shape), a mantra, etc. Therefore, if we wish to decrease the quantity of thoughts and distractions occuring in our field of awareness, it is necessary to practice some form of dharana (concentration).   Dharana practice does not end after our formal seated meditation ends each day. It is something that we must practice throughout our normal day to day lives. For example, my Guru instructed me to try and keep my attention and awareness in the frontal lobes of the brain at all times throughout the day to remain objective, discerning, creative, and disciplined. In doing so, one can remove their attention and prana from the reptilian brain that is responsible for fear, as well as primal cravings and drives. Mr. Davis also taught me that it was perfectly acceptable to practice pranayama or mantra at any time during the day when I needed to be more loving, relaxed, centered, clear, and objective. This radically shifted my understanding of dharana.   It is not only practiced on the meditation cushion, but it is something that must be practiced consistently during our mundane activities and routines as well.

When   we   have   our   attention   concentrated   on   something single-pointedly, this means that all else falls away. For example, during the practice of mantra, we ideally want to have our attention focused completely on the repetition of the sacred vibration.   In this case, there is only the mantra; all else falls away and we experience ourselves as fully present with the mantra. The mantra becomes a protective cocoon for the mind and reduces the quantity of thoughts appearing as mental vrittis that normally distract our attention. Therefore, distractions and obstacles do not exist for us when our attention is fully concentrated on a mantra. Distractions and obstacles are held at bay by the purifying force of the mantra. "Man" comes from manas, which essentially means mind, and "tra" is usually translated as tool or vehicle. Therefore, the mantra is the vehicle that *tra*nsports and navigates us around the obstacles and distractions of the river-like mind to the other shore, which is pure conscious awareness without distractions.

1.33 The clarification of our being comes about by cultivating attitudes of friendliness towards the happy, compassion for the unhappy, delight in the virtuous, and indifference toward the wicked.

This is one of the most important and famous verses in the Yoga Sutras of Patanjali. It is often quoted by yoga teachers when discussing issues of envy and jealousy. When we see others succeeding in any aspect of life, we should celebrate their success and be happy for them. Rather than envying the successful, we ought to aspire to be like them. The difference between jealousy and aspiration is paramount and should not be underestimated on the path to spiritual freedom. Institutions and organizations would be wise to encourage the values of aspiration and hard work, rather than the values of victimization and envy. The former promotes strength and courage, while the latter promotes weakness and hatred.

Compassion for the unhappy is also of the utmost importance for a yogi. This naturally begins to occur as our sadhana progresses. Long-term meditators tend to experience much more compassion for others than do non-meditators generally speaking. This is because compassion is an organically occuring side-effect or by-product of long-term meditation. As we strip ourselves of ourselves over the years, our true nature begins to shine through more and more. Therefore, the more we meditate effectively, the more we abide as the Self, which is inherently loving and compassionate. Also, as yogis, we should always strive to practice Karma Yoga, which is the yoga of selfless service and action in the world. In doing so, we act from our higher nature and avoid the pitfalls of acting from our ego.

"Delight in the virtuous" essentially refers to the love that we ought to have for the virtuous amongst us, especially the Guru(s). The reader should take note of the language used here. Patanjali does not say in this verse that we need to worship the virtuous; only that we should have "delight in the virtuous." The Guru is not to be worshipped. They are to be admired, loved, and cherished, but never worshipped. To worship something is to admit separation in between the worshipper and the object of worship. This separation is an illusion, as we discover in Nirvikalpa Samadhi. Therefore, yogis do not worship anything or anyone. However, it is perfectly acceptable and noble to find delight in one's Guru.

"Indifference toward the wicked" might be the most difficult of Patanjali's recommended attitudes for us to cultivate. My Guru had an important conversation with his Guru, Paramahansa Yogananda, a few weeks before his transition at his desert retreat center in Twentynine Palms, California in 1952. In this particular instance, Yogananda read my Guru's mind, as he often did, and answered Guruji's question without him having to ask it. He said at the time, "Don't worry about what others do or don't do. Don't look to the left or the right. Look straight ahead towards the goal and go all the way in your current lifetime. You can do it!" Guruji had been concerned at the time about the actions of others and was mildly mentally disturbed when Yogananda gave him this specific teaching. It is essentially the same as Patanjali's teaching in this verse. When we see injustice, we can play a small role in correcting the injustice as long as it comes from a place of peace, love, and compassion. However, this is hardly ever the case. Most people act out of ego, anger, envy, and judgement when it comes to issues of social injustice. We can not expect to assist others in their quest for equality, peace, and freedom if we are not experiencing internal equanimity, peace, and freedom. Indeed, we must "be the change" that we wish to see in the world.

1.34 Or, by the exhalation and retention of the breath.

The information regarding specific pranayama techniques in all of the ancient yoga texts is ambiguous and cryptic. What is being described here is a pranayama technique that was most likely well known during Patanjali's time and did not require further explanation. The same can be said for the pranayamas that are described in the Bhagavad Gita and other ancient yoga texts. Therefore, we are forced to interpret the wording and phraseology of the ancient authors based upon conjecture and speculation. However, we can speak generally here about pranayama in broad terms. Pranayama, or the expansion and movement of prana via breathing techniques, is used to relax the vrittis occuring in the body, astral body, and mind. It should be practiced before meditation to prepare the body, astral body, and mind for tranquil states of transcendence. In my tradition of Kriya Yoga, a very specific and somewhat complicated technique known as Kriya Pranayama is taught. It is the most effective and powerful pranayama technique for calming and pacifying vrittis known to yogis.

1.35 Or, the mind is held steady by concentration on a sense object.

Patanjali is offering a few basic methods for calming the vrittis in our being in these verses. He does a much better job of explaining all the methods in their appropriate order and sequence in the second section of the sutras. One such method is to concentrate on an object of the senses, such as the corresponding sensations that occur as we breathe. Generally, one is taught to concentrate their attention on the flow of air at the tip of the nose that occurs naturally with each breath. Every time our attention is distracted by vrittis, we can return our attention to the breath with minimal effort. This is an excellent technique to practice, especially for beginners, as they learn how to concentrate their minds for the first time. Another useful technique is to stare at a candle flame with open eyes as a means of concentration. These are but two examples, but we are free to choose any sense object upon which to concentrate our attention in an attempt to calm vrittis.

1.36 Or, by concentrating one's attention on the jyoti, which is beyond sorrow.

Another excellent technique, albeit a far more advanced one, is to concentrate on the jyoti, or inner light, that one sees in the forehead (ajna chakra) while practicing meditation. This is considered an advanced technique of dharana (concentration) because most people do not see an inner light when they meditate, especially in the beginning. However, with practice, one is usually capable of perceiving an inner light during refined superconscious states. This light changes color and brilliance depending upon the state of our brain and nervous system, as well as our energetic/emotional state. However, there are three colors that are typically seen more than any others: blue, white, and gold. Needless speculation regarding the meaning of each color is a waste of time and energy. One should simply observe the light calmly and objectively and gently attempt to merge their attention fully with it.

1.37 Or, by the practice of non-attachment to objects.

Vrittis can be pacified by the practice of dispassionate non-attachment. Desire for the objects of the senses produces a state of restlessness in which one is not at peace until a particular desire has been fulfilled. The state of restlessness caused by desires is antithetical to the practice of yoga, which has as its goal a state of permanent peace and contentment. Therefore, yogis should live a simple and humble lifestyle free from desires and the subsequent restlessness that follows. Desires come about because we identify with that which desires (the false self). The only permanent solution to the problems associated with desires is complete Self-realization. When we no longer identify ourselves with a person who has desires, we are free. We can then live from a "place" of peace, contentment, and love where desires are rendered utterly powerless.

1.38 Or, by the knowledge of dream and sleep states.

One should regularly contemplate the various states of consciousness that they typically experience on a day to day basis such as the dream state and the deep sleep state. In doing so, one is able to realize themselves as the objective, clear, peaceful observer of all changing, vibratory phenomena. It matters not what is occurring on the surface levels; at the deepest core of our being, we are ever unchanging, peaceful, loving, objective, and clear. The more we merge our attention fully with our essence, the less we identify with the changing nature of the mind and the more we abide as the Self.

During lucid dreams, we are conscious that what we are experiencing is a dream, and not real. Enlightenment is a lot like lucid dreaming because when we awaken spiritually, we view the universe of form as a dream. We realize that we were sleeping/dreaming through life all along, and we no longer give so much importance to the universe of form. When we awaken spiritually, we awaken from the dream of life and we are no longer subject to the happenings occurring within the grand illusion of maya. Following our awakening, we are able to view all vibratory phenomena through the same objective lens without reaction, judgement, participation, or identification. In other words, we see the universe as it is without the mental filters that tune us into frequencies of illusion and deception.

1.39 Or, by meditation upon the desired outcome.

The desired outcome of meditation is samadhi. Therefore, it is useful to contemplate what it would be like to experience samadhi. Furthermore, it is useful to contemplate what it would be like to be fully enlightened and liberated.   In doing so, one attracts the experience.   Our lived experience is greatly influenced by our thoughts. Our thoughts attract experiences into our lives that vibrate at the same frequency as the thoughts.   Therefore, if we are consistently contemplating the Divine, we are far more likely to experience It. Likewise, if our mind dwells on negativity, we are more likely to attract negative experiences into our lives. There exists a Divine universal mind that is responsive to our individualized mind. Our thoughts become our reality based upon universal laws of attraction/repulsion. Just as laws of cause and effect are universally obeyed in the physical dimension, so are they obeyed in the more subtle energetic and mental dimensions as well. We should aim to convert our minds into magnets for sattva, positivity, peace, and enlightened states of consciousness. The first piece of advice that Yogananda ever gave my Guru was, "Read a little, meditate more, think of God all the time." If we can reach a stage in our spiritual evolution where we are capable of truly "thinking of God all the time," then we will most assuredly attract the blessings and grace of the Divine into our lives.

1.40   The mastery of this extends from the smallest particle to the entire universe.

Dhyana, which essentially means uninterrupted thought-free concentration, allows us to experience pure, tranquil consciousness without its vibratory modifiers. Pure consciousness has no bounds. I believe that Patanjali is attempting to describe the boundlessness of pure consciousness in this verse by describing the mastery of dhyana as extending from the smallest object in the universe to the entire universe itself. It is a sort of analogy for describing the vast infinitude of pure consciousness.

1.41   Just as the pure crystal assumes the colors of objects placed near it, so the mind, with its diminished vrittis, can experience itself as the experiencer, the experience, or what is experienced. This is samadhi.

Oneness consciousness allows the mind to identify itself with the objects of its contemplation. Just as a clear crystal changes color based upon the color of the object placed behind it, our mind has the capacity to experience itself as an object. Mind is non-local. This means that it is only by happenstance that one's mind happens to be identified with a particular body, personality, and ego. We can learn, through advanced meditation techniques, to experience ourselves as other people, or even as inanimate objects by transferring our mind into the body of another person or into any desired object. We can, in essence, become one with an experiencer (ourselves or someone else), an experience, or an object of experience. However, all three are examples of an inferior stage of samadhi (savitarka samapatti) and require a support of one kind or another. In the higher, more refined stages of samadhi, there is a kind of oneness, which is not dependent upon anything. In other words, it is not oneness with something...it is simply oneness.

1.42 There, in savitarka samapatti, awareness is blended with words, concepts, and knowledge.

Savitarka samapatti is samadhi with support as described in the previous verse. When we experience ourselves as something other than what we are normally identified with, this is an experience of savitarka samapatti. The experience of oneness with something is useful, but it is not ultimately transformative. This preliminary stage of samadhi provides us with an invaluable experience of initiatory ego-loss, but it is not a direct experience of our true, highest nature.

1.43 Upon the purification of impressions, devoid of qualities, it shines forth as the object alone. This is nirvirarka.

Nirvitarka is a superior stage of samadhi whereby we experience our true nature and Ultimate Reality as one and the same (atman = Brahman). This rare experience is the goal of our daily yoga and meditation practice. During other planetary ages, it was a much more common experience for seekers to have. We currently live in a relatively dense age where nirvitarka samadhi is incredibly rare. However, it is very much a real experience, and not just something written down in an old book that people could only experience thousands of years ago.

The atman, or soul, has no qualities insofar as it has no form. However, we can attempt to describe it as being infinite, boundless, loving, peaceful, still, objective, and clear, but this description falls far short. These words are merely pointers that guide us to an experience of the soul, but the words are not substitutes for the experience itself. An intellectual understanding of spiritual matters is important and useful, but ultimately we must *experience* that which we wish to know.

In the experience of nirvitarka samadhi there is no subject or object...no separation. There is no identification with a body/mind/personality composite. There is no identification with anything for that matter. In nirvitarka, we realize that everything in the manifest universe is conscious and everything is the same. We realize that there is only oneness/sameness and that we are that. We experience ourselves as everything and nothing in the same moment...an intellectual paradox that only makes sense during the experience. In fact, following the experience of nirvitarka, nothing from the experience makes sense intellectually. When we try and explain the experience to others afterwards (as I am attempting to do now), we inevitably fail.

I used to believe that the spiritual path ended with nirvitarka samadhi. Now, however, I have come to realize that the spiritual path does not really begin until one has experienced nirvitarka. This is because, prior to the experience, we have no real knowledge of the soul and/or Ultimate Reality. Afterwards, we do have real knowledge of the soul and Ultimate Reality. Therefore, how can we claim to be on a spiritual path if we have no knowledge of spirit? It is only after we have gained knowledge of spirit that our true spiritual path actually begins. Prior to nirvitarka, one moves through the world as a blind person, unable to see. After nirvitarka, we have "eyes to see" and "ears to hear" as Jesus states in the Gospel of Thomas...we are finally freed from the blinders that have kept us fumbling around in spiritual ignorance for countless numbers of incarnations.

Many inexperienced spiritual teachers in the yoga tradition claim that the goal of the spiritual path is "permanent samadhi." For anyone who has ever experienced nirvitarka samadhi, there is the clear understanding that any notion of a permanent stage of nirvitarka is impossible if we wish to survive in our body/mind/personality composite on planet Earth. It is impossible to function normally while in nirvitarka...the ecstasy is too intense and enveloping and there is no identification with anything. Eating, walking, talking, and other normal day to day activities are rendered impossible during an experience of nirvitarka. Also, during very refined stages of nirvitarka, one's breathing stops for a time. We have the example of enlightened saints such as Anandamayi Ma who needed help in her early life with simple mundane activities like eating and walking due to her deep samadhi ecstasy. Likewise, in my own lineage, Yogananda had a specific protocol that his disciples were to follow in order to bring him back from nirvitarka so that he could function normally again. To be honest, I too have experienced nirvitarka on a number of occasions during which time I was unable to walk, talk, eat and perform normal functions and I have experienced prolonged periods in the breathless state where my body was in a sort of stasis that is difficult to explain. There exist many misguided spiritual teachers who think that anyone who claims to have experienced this type of rapture is exaggerating or lying. This is because they have never experienced it, and therefore they believe (due to an inflated ego) that if they have never experienced it, it must not be real. I assure you that nirvitarka is real. It is an experience of complete Divine union in which the rapture is so intense that the performance of normal mundane activities becomes futile.

On the spiritual path, there is life before nirvitarka, and life after. Prior to our experience of nirvitarka, we live as if in a dream. After nirvitarka, we know (not believe) ourselves to be spiritual beings who temporarily inhabit forms for the purposes of growth, evolution, and awakening. Prior to nirvitarka, we are always striving towards enlightenment, as though there were anywhere to go or anything to do. After nirvitarka, the striving ends, though there is still work to be done to clean up active and latent karma. Prior to nirvitarka, the Divine is a mental construct. After nirvitarka, the Divine is a lived experience. Nirvitarka is, in essence, enlightenment. However, this experience does not last. It may last a few seconds, minutes, or even days sometimes, but ultimately we return to our identification with the temporary, limited self as a survival mechanism.

There are a few rare souls who have remained in a state of nirvitarka for days or weeks who allowed their bodies to die as they consciously dissolved themselves. I am certain that this has occurred, but the few cases of this throughout human history must be incredibly isolated and rare. Typically the subconscious mind leads us back into our previous identification with the false self so that the body can continue to live and function in the physical plane. Most of us are simply not ready to dissolve forever into the formless void, which is the absolute highest stage of spiritual evolution known as kaivalya, or final liberation. Typically, we must first ascend through various astral incarnations as we continue our spiritual evolution in the higher subtle dimensions unencumbered by the hindrances of a physical body. Following that, we shed the emotional pranamaya kosha or astral sheath and we continue our evolution in the causal planes as mind-stuff. Eventually, the mind is no longer necessary and we are free to relinquish our individuality as we merge and dissolve into formlessness. We are unaware of any souls who have dissolved because they do not return to talk about it, but I am certain that it has occurred.

1.44   If the object of concentration is of a subtle nature, these two states of samadhi are known as savichrara and nirvichara.

Savichara is a contemplative practice. For example, if one wishes to understand a mysterious metaphysical reality, they can merge their attention and awareness fully with that which they wish to contemplate in order to experience illuminating insights and revelations. This is a more active form of samadhi in which the meditator is intentionally attempting to experience union with a specific contemplative object in order to gain insight into that object. This advanced technique should be reserved for accomplished yogis who have already experienced the other stages of samadhi and who wish to gain valuable insights into the inner workings of the universe and the Divine. For one who has not already experienced the other stages of samadhi, this practice does not bear fruit. However, for one who is accomplished in samadhi, meditative contemplation has the potential to reveal the occulted secrets and mysteries of the mind of God.

Nirvichara is a much deeper contemplative practice where the meditator wishes to contemplate the pure essence of the Divine. For the extremely advanced and rare yogi who is able to maintain prolonged states of nirvitarka samadhi, they are free to further contemplate the Divine and probe ever deeper.

1.45 The subtlety of objects extends to the unmanifest.

Everything within the manifest realm blossoms and unfolds from the unmanifest. How this is possible, no one really knows for sure. This is why many of the North American shamanic traditions refer to God correctly only as "Great Mystery." In the philosophy of Samkhya, speculative attempts are made to try and explain how "something can come from nothing." However, these attempts are a waste of time. It is of little value to speculate about such things. Even the wisest enlightened masters with personal insights on the matter have failed to convey whatever limited understanding they may have of the processes of cosmic manifestation and unfoldment in a logical, understandable way that the rest of us can comprehend. The great religious traditions of the world all have their own creation myths and stories, which also do little to help us understand how the material ultimately came from the immaterial. The scientists of our day have largely convinced themselves that the big bang theory is scientific fact. Nonetheless, the big bang theory does not explain the primary cause of manifestation; at best, it is a feeble attempt to explain only the effect.

There is an excellent parable from the Buddhist tradition that succinctly explains the futility of wasteful metaphysical speculation. The parable starts off by telling the story of a man wounded by an arrow. He needs a surgeon to remove the arrow immediately in order for him to survive. However, he frantically begins asking those around him for information about his assailant and his whereabouts rather than having his wound attended to. When told that he must seek out a surgeon to remove the arrow, he responds by stating that he will not have the arrow removed until he knows all the information that he is seeking beforehand. The spiritual path is like this for many intellectual seekers. They wish to try and understand every detail of spiritual and metaphysical philosophy while they do nothing to end their suffering. Wasting time on philosophical speculation, especially as it concerns creation, is not the most practical use of our time. Once one has stabilized themselves fully in Self-realization, they are free to pursue these philosophical matters because they have already removed the arrow of ignorance and suffering. However, the rest of us would be wise to prioritize more time in superconscious meditation and less time trying to figure it all out.

1.46 These samadhis occur with seeds.

One who still has seeds or samskaras is capable of experiencing the previously mentioned stages of samadhi. However, the fewer samskaras one has, the easier it is to experience the more refined stages. In other words, one need not be seedless to experience samadhi. What is being described by Patanjali here is a stage of spiritual development and not a specific experiential state of samadhi. With repeated and frequent experiences of samadhi, one can neutralize their samskaras and prevent the accumulation of future samskaras. Therefore, according to Patanjali it is possible to reach a stage of spiritual development whereby all samskaras have been neutralized and is therefore considered the seedless stage of spiritual development, which Patanjali describes in verse 51.

1.47 Proficiency in nirvichara results in spiritual clarity.

Proficiency in experiencing samadhi states results in ever increasing levels of spiritual enlightenment.

1.48   There, prajna is truth-bearing.

In samadhi, prajna (wisdom) is gained due to the experience of the truth of one's being during the experience. All other wisdom pales in comparison to that which is gained via samadhi. One might possess all of the world's knowledge and remain completely ignorant. There are many brilliant PhD level scientists who smugly pretend to know it all, and yet know nothing of their true nature or the nature of Ultimate Reality...they live their entire lives in a sort of callow oblivion even though they are worshipped by our modern technological society as "geniuses."

1.49   It is different from the wisdom gained via tradition or inference because it is of a higher order.

The wisdom gained via spiritual and religious teachings and scriptures and/or the wisdom gained via inference are inferior to that wisdom which is gained via direct experience of the Divine in samadhi. Prior to one's enlightenment, sacred texts and scriptures are of the utmost importance in one's path and sadhana. However, after we begin to experience the profound and refined stages of samadhi, words no longer hold as much meaning for us. After our awakening, we realize that words are mere pointers that guide us to an experience. However, once we have the experience, the pointers are no longer necessary. It is like someone who needs to use a map to reach a new destination. They may need to use the map several times until they become accustomed to the route. However, once they have reached their destination and they know how to get there again and again, the map is no longer necessary. After samadhi, words become superfluous and unnecessary on one's path. However, many yogis with an intellectual predilection continue to study spiritual philosophy and sacred texts following their experiences of samadhi, but their study of the texts is no longer a search for truth. Truth can only be reached via samadhi.

1.50 The samskaras produced from that neutralize other samskaras.

The beneficial samskaras produced from samadhi experiences neutralize other samskaras. Samskaras, or karmic seeds, must grow in the ego-field. The reactions, judgements, and identifications of the ego (ahamkara) become the fertile soil out of which our samskaras sprout and flourish. In samadhi, there is no ego-field for the seeds to take root in. They have nowhere to grow. The soul is immaterial; consequently, it can not accommodate anything which is material. Samskaras, while subtle, do have a material vibratory reality.

The soul has no karma or samskaras. In the Western religious traditions, it is taught that humans are wretched sinners at their core. In stark contrast, the yoga tradition teaches us that, at our core, we are clear and stainless. In other words, the soul has no taint or original sin...it is forever pure. Salvation is unnecessary since we are already pure and Divine. All that is necessary is the unveiling of our true nature. Yoga is the means for this unveiling.

Samadhi experiences leave a residue in our being that endures. This residue (samskara) is difficult to put into terms that can be easily understood by someone who has not had a samadhi experience.

1.51 Samadhi results in the cessation of all seeds, even this one.

"Nirbija samadhi" (the terminology used in this verse) does not describe a particular temporary state of samadhi or type of samadhi. Instead, it refers to a very advanced permanent stage of spiritual development that occurs via frequent experiences of samadhi in which all samskaras (even the ones gained from samadhi experiences mentioned in the previous verse) have been neutralized and the possibility of accumulating future samskaras has been eliminated. Very few yogis, if any, ever reach this stage of spiritual development where they no longer possess samskaras, especially while incarnated in a human form on planet Earth. Typically, one must spend time working in the more subtle astral and causal planes following their ascension to completely eradicate all samskaras from their being. I believe that Patanjali is essentially describing a theoretical stage of spiritual development (jivanmukta), rather than a realistic stage of spiritual development that one can expect to attain while incarnated on this particular planet during this particular age. However, as my own personal journey has shown me time and again, anything is possible, and as Paramahansa Yogananda often said, "You must erase the word impossible from your mind."

About the Author

Rev. Christopher Sartain is an authorized and ordained teacher in the Kriya Yoga tradition. He was ordained by his Guru, Roy Eugene Davis, in July 2012. Christopher is the director of Kriya Yoga Chile Ashram, a retreat center located in the southern Andes Mountains. He is also the spiritual director of Vinyasa Yoga Chile, a yoga school with more than 300 graduates of its 200 and 300 hour yoga teacher training programs. Christopher is the author of several books including *The Sacred Science of Yoga and the Five Koshas*.

For all inquiries, please write to:
chrissartain@gmail.com

Please visit the following websites for more information about Christopher and his offerings:
www.kriyayogachile.com
www.vinyasayogachile.cl
www.koshasbook.com
www.youtube.com/kriyayogi